PUFFIN BOOKS is part of the Penguin Random House group of companies
whose addresses can be found at global.penguinrandomhouse.com.

First published 2016
Copyright © Victoria and Albert Museum, London
Illustrated by Marcus Walters. The moral right of the illustrator has been asserted
Printed in Slovakia   001
ISBN: 978–0–141–37413–0

Picture credits

Endpapers
Furnishing fabric, Hilary Rosenthal for
Bernard Wardle & Co, UK, 1966.
V&A: CIRC.4-1967

Fashion
Man's suit, Mr Fish, UK, about 1968.
V&A: T.310&A-1979
Minidress, Paul Babb and Pamela
Proctor for Twiggy Dresses, London, UK,
1967–1969. V&A: T.15-2007
Rock and pop costume, unknown, UK,
1967. V&A: S.983-1982
Minidress, Biba, London, UK, 1967.
V&A: T.12-1982

A Trend Transformation
Miniskirt and belt, Dispo, London, UK,
1967. V&A: T.175 to B-1986
Twiggy, Ronald Traeger, UK, 1967
© Ronald Traeger, 1967
Biba label, John McConnell, London, UK,
1960s to 1970s. V&A: E.3681-1983

Music
Bob Dylan album insert, Milton Glaser,
New York, USA, 1967 © Milton Glaser,
1967

Woodstock Festival poster image
provided courtesy of Woodstock Ventures
LLC. WOODSTOCK and the Dove-and-
Guitar Logo are registered trademarks of
Woodstock Ventures LLC. Poster design
by Arnold Skolnick.
Sgt. Pepper's Lonely Hearts Club Band
record cover, Peter Blake and Jann
Haworth, UK, 1967 © Apple Corps Ltd.
UFO Mk II poster, Hapshash and the
Coloured Coat, designed by Nigel
Waymouth and Michael English, UK,
1967. V&A: S.47-1978

Records in Rebellion
Photo of Woodstock, Elliot Landy, USA,
1969 © Elliot Landy/Getty Images
Beatles 'All You Need Is Love'
photograph, 1967 © David Magnus/Rex/
Shutterstock
Pye Model 1108 radio, Robin Day for
Pye Ltd, Cambridge, UK, 1966.
V&A: CIRC.394-1967
Jimi Hendrix, PHOTOGRAPH BY
GERED MANKOWITZ © BOWSTIR
Ltd. 2016/Mankowitz.com

Protest
War is Not Healthy for Children and
Other Living Things poster, Lorraine
Schneider for Another Mother for Peace
Inc., USA, 1968. V&A: E.321-2004
Unite To Fight poster, Su Negrin and
Inkworks Press, USA, 1976.
V&A: E.152-2011

Our Time is Now!
Martin Luther King Jr. 'Dream' Speech,
Agence France Presse, USA, 1963
© Agence France Presse/Getty Images
Earth Day 1960, unknown, New York,
USA, 1970 © Hulton Archive/Getty
Images
Demonstrators at the Miss America
Pageant, unknown, New Jersey, USA,
1968 © Bettmann/Getty Images

Home
Observer magazine cover, Maureen Gree
and Adrian Flowers, London, UK, 1968.
V&A: PP.38.A © Maureen Green and
Adrian Flowers/Observer
Apollo 11 Moon landing, NASA, 1968
© NASA

New Ways to Live
Whole Earth Catalog, Stewart Brand,
USA, 1968 © Stewart Brand

Technology
Earth Rise, NASA, 1968 © NASA

YOU SAY YOU WANT A
REVOLUTION?

THE SWINGING SIXTIES HAS ARRIVED. IT'S THE START OF A REVOLUTION!

DEAR READER,

Most of the 60s and early 70s designs you see in this book were considered REBELLIOUS. We are so lucky today to be free with our ideas – a freedom that many of us take for granted!

In the 1960s we battled to be recognized as independent, freethinking individuals by our parents. We were still under the strict Victorian rules, where children should be seen and not heard. But BIBA stood to change all that. In our first BIBA shop, mothers did not dare even enter the front door!

The walls of the shop were painted dark purple; the drapes were drawn covering what would normally be a window display, and the music played intensely loud. The music was unusual – the Beatles, the Rolling Stones, The Kinks and many other sounds that were strange to adults.

Rock 'n' roll was how the young London crowd broke free of old rules. They could wear what they liked and listen to that wicked music all night. It was all about new sounds, new styles and new-found freedom. The skirts got shorter and shorter, and trouser suits were banned from hotels. Cathy McGowan, presenter of the brilliant READY STEADY GO! music programme, made the front page of the newspapers when she was banned from entering the Savoy Hotel for wearing such an outfit.

It all seems so hilarious today and difficult to understand how Victorian the mood was during that time. It seems time stood still after the war, but the 1960s changed everything . . .

Barbara Hulanicki

Barbara Hulanicki OBE is a fashion designer, style icon and founder of hip 1960s fashion emporium BIBA.

FASHION

60s fashion has arrived in a psychedelic explosion of colour and excitement! Style-conscious shoppers in bell-bottom jeans, miniskirts and sharp suits flock to boutiques to listen to pop music and try on all the latest trends. From the clean-cut style of the mods to the long hair and carefree attitude of the hippies, looks evolve at lightning speed. The eyes of the fashion world are moving away from Parisian runways towards everyday street style as young designers revolutionize clothing.

HAIR TODAY

Pop

A TREND TRANSFORMATION

Disposable **PAPER CLOTHING** was a new 60s trend. People tried wearing paper dresses, paper skirts, paper suits and even paper underwear!

With her cropped hair and heavy eye make-up, London-born model **TWIGGY** became 'The Face of '66' at the age of 16! Many consider her to be the world's very first supermodel.

As the owner of 15 shops on Carnaby Street in London, menswear designer John Stephen was nicknamed 'The King of Carnaby Street'. Stephen, along with designers like Michael Fish, fuelled a trend for colourful, patterned, flamboyant menswear – a trend now called **'THE PEACOCK REVOLUTION'**.

Barbara Hulanicki's first **BIBA** boutiques sold trendy, inexpensive clothes and were decorated with Victorian antiques. The biggest store had an exotic roof garden (complete with flamingos!) where Biba threw extravagant, star-studded parties.

MINISKIRTS:
THE HEMLINE INDEX

In the 1920s, economist George Taylor suggested that there was a link between the economy and the lengths of skirts – the shorter the skirt, the better the economy. Short skirts were popular with 'flapper' girls during the boom of the 1920s, and again in the 60s when people had more money to spend on clothes after the Second World War. With their radically short styles, designers Mary Quant and André Courrèges brought back the miniskirt in a big way!

MUSIC

From funk and soul to rock 'n' roll, all kinds of music hit the charts. Radically new sounds from the Beatles and the Rolling Stones are part of a boom in 'pop music'. Bands draw on a variety of styles, including rock, jazz, beat music, dance and country. Teens no longer listen to the same music as their parents, but spend hours discovering new bands in record shops and listening to borrowed LPs at home. Songs like The Who's 'My Generation' and Bob Dylan's 'The Times They Are A-Changin' become a universal language for the 60s revolution.

LATEST RELEASES →

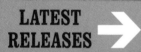
HI FI

JAZZ
It's time to find out where it's at...

TRIP OUT

DREAM SPACE
THE NEW IN SOUND FROM OUT THERE

FREE PEACE FESTIVAL
DOLORES PARK · SAN FRANCISCO
SATURDAY 12 JUNE 1967

SURF'S UP!
HERE COME THE BEACH BOYS
BUY THEIR NEW ALBUM
TODAY!

BOB DYLAN

LIVE IN CONCERT
THE KINKS
PLAYING ALL THEIR LATEST HITS
THURS. 14 MARCH
THE TOWN HALL

WOODSTOCK
MUSIC & ART FAIR
presents

AN
AQUARIAN
EXPOSITION
in
WHITE LAKE, N.Y.

WITH

3 DAYS
of PEACE
& MUSIC

AUGUST
15, 16, 17.

LISTENING BOOTH

DYLAN

UFO

PSYCHEDELIC
MUSICAL
HAPPENINGS

AT THE TOWN HALL
FIRST FRIDAY OF
EVERY MONTH

FREE
PEACE
FESTIVA

DELORES PARK - SAN FRANCI
SATURDAY 12, JUNE 1967

RECORDS IN REBELLION

Four days. 32 acts. 600 acres. 500,000 people. The famous **WOODSTOCK** open-air music festival in August 1969 was held on a dairy farm in New York State. With unforgettable performances from musicians such as Jimi Hendrix and Joan Baez, it is considered by *Rolling Stone* magazine to be one of the top 50 moments that changed rock 'n' roll.

THE BEATLES were a group of four young lads from Liverpool, England – Paul McCartney, John Lennon, Ringo Starr and George Harrison. Their performance of 'All You Need Is Love' in 1967 was part of the world's first live global satellite television broadcast. Over 400 million people tuned in to watch!

In the 60s, most fans of pop and rock 'n' roll would tune into 'pirate' radio stations. These unauthorized stations broadcast contemporary music from ships on international waters to bypass strict UK broadcasting laws. By 1967, around 15 million listeners were tuning into **PIRATE RADIO** every day!

One of the world's greatest guitar heroes, **JIMI HENDRIX** was known for his wild performance style, which included playing his guitar behind his back, upside down and even with his teeth!

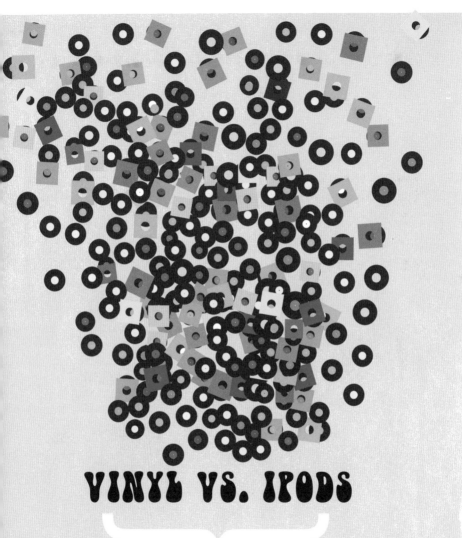

VINYL VS. IPODS

An iPod today might hold 40,000 songs. A vinyl album usually has around 12 tracks on it.

Carrying around your music collection in the 60s would not have been easy!

PROTEST

The most radical revolution of all is the one happening in people's minds! From London to San Francisco, ordinary people take to the streets to voice revolutionary ideas. It's the 60s and in the UK it is legal for a woman to be paid less than a man for doing the same job, and illegal to be homosexual. People are protesting against these terrible political and social injustices, and demanding the right to live alternative lifestyles. This growing counterculture campaigns for civil and gay rights, freedom of speech, peace, the environment and more. This is their time to bring about a revolution!

BAN THE BOMB
PEACE
UNITE TO FIGHT!
JUNE 28/ DAY OF SOLIDARITY WITH GAY STRUGGLES
EQUALITY FOR ALL

OUR TIME IS NOW!

The **CIVIL RIGHTS MOVEMENT** in the 60s was a collection of several groups with different methods, all fighting for equal rights for black people. Protestors faced a difficult choice between the peaceful forms of resistance championed by Dr Martin Luther King Jr. and more violent forms of protest used by organizations like the Black Panther Party.

In 1963, Dr Martin Luther King Jr. spoke out for equal rights for black Americans in his famous speech, **'I HAVE A DREAM'**. The day before the speech, the expensive sound system that was hired for the event was sabotaged. Luckily, the Attorney General and U.S. senator-to-be Robert Kennedy enlisted the Army Corps of Engineers to fix it overnight!

Young American men protested against fighting in the Vietnam War by burning the draft cards that the government sent to call them to action. The practice was made illegal in 1965, although very few people were convicted. Other **ANTI-VIETNAM WAR** protestors stuck carnations into gun barrels, leading American poet Allen Ginsberg to coin the term 'flower power'.

Annual **GAY PRIDE** marches on 28 June commemorate the Stonewall uprising – a key moment that united the gay liberation movement in America. On the same day in 1969, there was a violent police raid at the Stonewall Inn, a bar in New York City that was popular with members of the gay community, and a series of spontaneous riots started in protest. Homosexuality was decriminalized in several countries in the 60s and 70s.

Environmental concern built through the decade, and on 22 April 1970, around 20 million Americans participated in demonstrations for a healthy environment at the very first **EARTH DAY**. By the end of the year, the United States Environmental Protection Agency was founded and the Clean Air, Clean Water and Endangered Species acts were passed.

Around 400 feminists protested at the Miss America beauty pageant in 1968. They threw false eyelashes, bras and high-heeled shoes into a 'freedom trash can' and held up placards that said 'Everybody Is Beautiful'. The phrase 'burn your bra' is often associated with the 60s **FEMINISM** movement, but there is no evidence that bras were burnt at any of the demonstrations.

HOME

Space-age furniture, groovy lava lamps, Victorian antiques and Art Nouveau-inspired artwork . . . the look of the average home in the 60s is a mix of the exciting future and nostalgia for the past. More and more products are being created and sold to customers who want new and modern appliances, like fridges and TVs. The desire for constant change has led to a trend for throwaway products. Disposable cardboard armchairs, inflatable furniture and paper clothing – it's all part of a new and daring attempt to imagine living differently!

OBSERVER

NEW WAYS TO LIVE

With a widespread throwaway attitude and an obsession with the 'new', the 60s has been nicknamed the **'DECADE OF DISPOSABILITY'**.

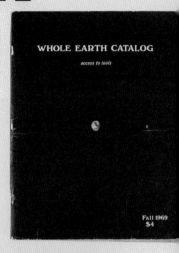

However, some people rejected the throwaway culture. The **WHOLE EARTH CATALOG** was started by American writer Stewart Brand and featured products – some of which were eco-friendly and build-it-yourself – that offered an alternative to those advertised on TV or sold in supermarkets. Many readers of the catalogue had moved out of cities to live sustainably in 'back-to-the-land' communities.

In the 60s there were only three **TV** channels to choose from in the UK, and all TV was shown in black and white. Colour television started to become available around 1967, but wasn't commonplace until the 70s.

England's win against Germany in the 1966 FIFA **WORLD CUP** is still Britain's most-watched TV broadcast ever – almost 33 million people tuned in to watch the game!

THE EVOLUTION OF THE TELEPHONE

Operator, please . . .

1880s

1920s

1960s

In the 60s most homes had telephones, but nobody had a mobile phone. The first handheld phone was invented in the 70s, but it looked very different from the sleek, powerful mobiles we have today.

1980s

1990s

2000s

c u l8r

:)

2010s

TECHNOLOGY

Technology is developing at lightning speed and groundbreaking inventions, such as colour television, the first handheld calculator and the first ATM or cash machine, are changing everyday life.

Air travel is no longer just for the rich and famous; with the development of the 'jumbo jet' and the invention of Concorde – an aeroplane that travels twice as fast as the speed of sound – this is a new age of tourism for all.

The most exciting developments, however, are happening out of this world: people have landed on the moon! From 16 July 1969, the Apollo 11 mission was broadcast live on television to music by Pink Floyd and David Bowie. Four days after lift-off, the astronauts landed: Neil Armstrong, Michael Collins and Buzz Aldrin. Armstrong stepped out of the landing craft and said the unforgettable words: 'That's one small step for man; one giant leap for mankind.'

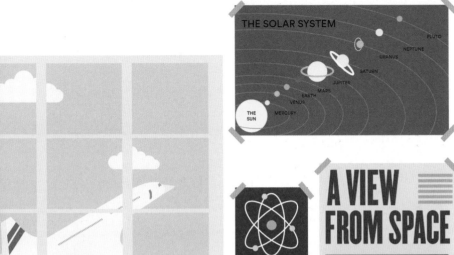

THE SOLAR SYSTEM

PLUTO

NEPTUNE

URANUS

SATURN

JUPITER

MARS

EARTH

VENUS

THE SUN

MERCURY

NUCLEAR
ENERGY OF THE FUTURE

A VIEW
FROM SPACE

THE SPACE RACE

1957 – Russian rocket **SPUTNIK 1** orbited the earth for three months.

1959 – The first successful non-manned spaceflight to the moon was made by US rocket **LUNA 2**.

1961 – Russian **YURI GAGARIN** became the first man in space, in the **VOSTOK 1** spacecraft.

1963 – **VALENTINA TERESHKOVA** was the first woman in space, in the **VOSTOK 6** spacecraft.

1965 – **ALEXEY LEONOV** made the first space walk.

1969 – **APOLLO 11** was the first mission to land men on the moon.

THE MOON is about 238,855 miles (384,400 km) away from the earth.

WHAT IS YOUR SWINGING SIXTIES PERSONA?

Follow the arrows that most sound like you

START HERE

I'm always on the hunt for cool new hangouts.

You'll find me exploring the great outdoors in my free time.

My music collection is full of pop albums by heroes like The Beatles and David Bowie.

My music collection is full of hits from rock 'n' roll legends like The Who and The Grateful Dead!

I always try to live in the moment.

I'm always daydreaming about the future.

the style in hair that hasn't been trimmed for months?

When it starts to get a bit chilly, a parka coat is my go-to jacket.

A classic leather jacket is the way to go. Mine has lots of zips and badges!

of magazines!

I reduce my carbon footprint by cycling everywhere I go!

My ideal ride is a big noisy motorbike.

change into for my next gig!

All of my clothes are right on trend – you won't catch me in anything from last season.

All of my clothes are 100% eco-friendly.

REBELLIOUS ROCKER

TRENDY MOD

FLOWER POWER HIPPY

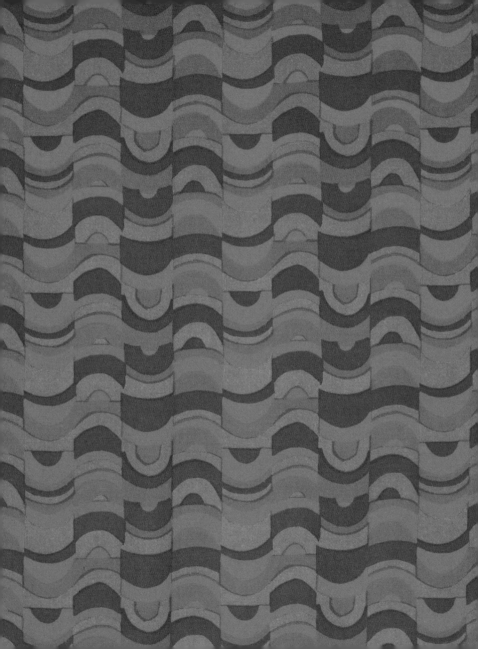